DISARMAMENT

Disarmament

JOHN TERPSTRA

GASPEREAU PRESS PRINTERS & PUBLISHERS MMIII

CONTENTS

Restoration

After the cigar factory, the valley of sugar fields
and the nineteenth-century Spanish mansion
built on slave labour, our guide led us
into the Iglesia Parroquial de la Santísima Trinidad.
I half-expect to hear a four-piece Cuban band strike up
as I tell how my daughter removes her peaked cap,
out of respect, she'll explain to a friend back home,
and we listen to the story of a wooden altar,
one of many into which are carved
precise moments in the life of the Virgin Mary.
A young woman saunters by our group.
She looks surprisingly like a prostitute,
and a moment later Katie confesses
that she's given the woman her hat.
She pointed. She wanted it. What could I do?

My daughter seems pleased to have given away
something of her own, in this country of few possessions
and little money, but the white baseball cap
is her souvenir gift of last year's vacation,
when we carried our most recent possession—
her unexpected news—with us
like a piece of baggage we must fit
into the compact model of our family,
and I am not so generous.

She gives me her permission to tell this,
If I can read it first, she says, and to add
that in the old, barely kept-up Cuban church
another carved Mary entertains a holy dove
which hovers over her head, reminding Katie

of the Advent Sunday morning we heard
about the young woman's pregnancy, its origins
in the divine, when she leaned over my shoulder
and whispered, *That's what happened to me.*

What a scandal, Katherine, to profane
the gospel story with a joke,
but I laughed, because it *was* funny,
and you seemed so at peace, finally,
with yourself and with your pregnancy,
I began to wonder if the truth was not
the telling of that unlikely story
within a building the story helped to build,
that gave you permission. If, in that precise
moment, your baby became your honour,
what would I contradict?

Exiting the iglesia of the parish of Trinidad, Cuba,
we pass a small box balanced on a single wooden leg
like a crutch, and an elderly man making
eye contact, who points to a slot in the box top
as he repeats the phrase,
For the restoration... For the restoration...
I check for singles in my wallet
as our guide explains fathers are forbidden
to wear their white collars on weekdays,
in this country of equals—
but all I can find is a twenty.

The maracas, ancient muted trumpet, drums
and two guitars of a five-piece band
play for us at dinner,
then move to entertain later diners
under the open plaza, who dance.
Mary and I are lying on the resort beach,
allowing the stars to reconcile
the disparities
as we list the known facts:
our teenage daughter offering the white-
winged, souvenir baseball cap
to a streetwalker who asks for it,
inside a church where the walls weep
stains of infiltrating rainwater, within sight
of an altar honouring the impossible event
we are not hesitant to believe true
for her too,
so low had been her estate.

It is the old man's role to keep up the place
where this happens, where the paths of the two
sister-leads of the gospel drama
cross, asking after restoration.

I wish I'd given him the twenty.

SAYING GOODNIGHT

Lying in your mother's bed, five hundred miles
from home, having come to see her
through her latest hospital stay,
you're feeling a little like a young blind puppy.
The ticking from her bedside timepiece
is louder, more richly mechanical than your own;
the rhythmic persistent push-pull, push-pull
of its internal clockwork,
that you imagine placing under the pillow.

Meanwhile, on the third floor ward, your mother
in her almost inaudible hospital voice,
says, "I want to go home."
Her finger, though, is pointing toward the ceiling;
an action that so quickly depletes her body's strength
the arm soon falls
to lie beside her where she lies beyond the comfort
of her eternal working heart's
persistent push and pull.

I'm lying with you in your mother's bed,
a disconnected appendage, and I want to go home too.
I'm restless and dreaming we're on the third floor deck
of the ferry crossing the Bay of Fundy.
Our centre of gravity here is somewhere below
and behind us, and we pivot, smooth and hugely,
on swells and plungers that pitch and tilt us
to radical angles, in a rhythm entirely irrhythmic,
unpredictable, that you'd never sleep a child to—
though it isn't unpleasant.

An obvious dream, I think, while dreaming it.
A great white wave tries to wake us, exploding
over the deck, and as the water pours down
the lounge windows, a woman your mother's vintage
labouriously stands, turns to her companion, and says,
"Unbelievable." And it is, in a manner of speaking.
She turns again, this time stepping toward the door,
and says she wants to see for herself
this ocean she and we and the Fundy ferry
are pushing through.

And turning in my dream of sleep as she turns to go,
I inadvertently assume the same position in which I saw
my father lie, half-curled against the bed-edge,
as if to enclose within himself the black the doctor said
he was so full of, blooming like phosphorescence.
Yet it seemed a kind of return, his sleeping shape.
It seemed so clear he was returning,
and that the place was hospitable he was returning to,
and this knowledge was contained within the pain-shaped form,
his unbetraying body.

I almost envied him his almost touching it,
the still and endless moment
when the moving vessel pulls to berth.

Goodnight Dad. Goodnight Mom. Goodnight
sweet sainted parents; mothers, fathers, all.
What more can you do than draw our fear away?
Goodnight.

And goodnight to all your parent's parents too.
You're not so complicated any longer, or taxed
by illness, age, infirmity, or us.
Goodnight.
Goodnight.

See you in the morning.

Trinity Sunday, Sydling St. Nicholas

—for Lee and Judy

Kneeling inside that stone parable of time and place,
  on the first morning of our walking vacation,
  there was little distance between ourselves
and the words unwinding from the Book of Common Prayer,
wending a dynamic of sense and sound
as physical as the down and bottom,
hill and tumulus we'd soon be tramping,
over the flint of close distinctions,
with such pleasure, and fearless, clear
as Sydling Water;
                    and the stone of expanding rings
dropped into the pond of that high day
was our observance of it,
there and then.

We nearly doubled the number of congregants,
but this enterprise has never been about numbers.
It is to kneel before the deepening connections
the eating and drinking make for us,
despite all breakings of time and place.
The silver chalice, tipped toward our mouths,
served in that house over four hundred years.
Eleven generations past, his grandfather,
whom Lee traced to this small village in Dorset,
also touched lips to rim.

Our last long walk that week, we crested a hill
and saw, carved into the edge of a stone bench,

NOTHING IS DISTANT FROM GOD

and sat and caught our breath,

　　　　　　　　　　drinking the view
and mouthing those fourth century words
of St. Monica, which echoed across the valley
and the past five days, and the living gap
of hundreds of miles, and the breaks of years
between the times we four
have come together,

　　　　　　　　here and now.

PLANETARY LIVES

Somewhere on the planet, the perfectly rounded
white nose of an aircraft faces you
through the plate glass window of the departure lounge,
and the jet turbine engine slows
until it appears no more portentous than a house fan,
unplugged,
as a supremely powerful machine
completes one journey,
and now will be readied to loft you on yours.

The past is revisitable.
You may return, physically, to the street or town,
the rural route of your raising.
It all looks the same, or it doesn't,
or its faithfulness to the facts of memory
hinges upon changes within your own landscape,
rather than on its recurrence
so close to your body.

Flying, driving, walking, you stand at last
in the middle of your old prairie schoolfield,
on the same day, coincidentally,
that senior citizen Glenn is lofting into the stratosphere
a second time, happy as a boy.

But the schoolyard isn't a field anymore.
New buildings fill its vast, open space.
The horizon has been raised, there is less sky.
The long-jump sandpit and the rectangular egg
of the boarded, outdoor skating rink are elsewhere,
while the tetherball pole no longer stands

near the door you blasted through
at the recess bell, to get there first,

to hand-bat the hanging ball
around the post it is tethered to the top of,
against the hand that wants to send it counterwise,
into ever-faster, shorter circles,
until the inflated orb pulls snug to the axis
of the foot-packed world, and stops.

I loved that game. It was something I was good at.
I loved the immediate, post-win unwinding of the ball,
pursuing its languorous momentum
in perfect, widening spirals of return.

It will occur to you, then, that your only connection
to the current landscape of your school age
is that you stood here also
on that day thirteen thousand rotations back
when the astronaut John Glenn first spun
three times around the earth.

You carry with you the first patch of ground
you intimately know each inch of
when you go,
                    where it is free to remain unchanged
as you travel on or off the planned trajectories,
observing from the tail-end of the thin thread that connects you,
a prairie river's no-hurry meander to Hudson,
how blue, from above, the whole planet appears—

how transfixingly lovelier, each time round.
And though you sense that your brief stay here
originates in some galactic elsewhere,
you may wish to remain,
seeking a place to touch down
as often as humanly possible.

GIANTS

There used to be giants,
and they loved it here. They'd sit
their giant hinds in a row along the top edge
of the escarpment, and pick at the loose rock
with their hands or their feet, then throw or skip
the smoothest stones across the bay, to see who could land one
on the sandstrip, three miles away;

or they'd spring themselves off the scarp top
like you would off a low wall, and go running
all the way to the end of the sandbar,
and jump across the water to the other side,
or jump in, splashing and yelling up the ravines,
chasing each other's echoes.

This was only a few thousand years ago,
and the giants were still excited about the glaciers,
which were just leaving; about not having to wear
their coats all the time, and what
the ice and water had done, shaping and carving
this gentle, wild landscape!

They loved it here.

I'm telling you, they absolutely loved
every living minute here,

and they regretted ever having to leave.

FLAGRANCE

Three yards over, a neighbour is breaking small bunches
of last year's weeds into the altar pan of his barbeque.
He pushes them down till the fire catches, then quick
draws back from its tender licking, laughing,
as his wife looks on,
                              and talks to their neighbour
on the other side, who's emerged into public view
for the first time since moving in, mid-winter,
and props himself by their fence post like an old hand,
inquiring after bylaws, garbage days,
                                          as a young daughter
caroms out the door with a boyfriend, slinging the lightweight
backpack of her beauty over a shoulder as she leaves
her *adieus* booming off the walls of the house,
abandoned,
                    and the three crones on lawn chairs nextdoor
intensify their verbal concoction with shrieks
of crow.

In spring's extending daylight, a coolness now returns.
Having lured our willing, grateful skins outdoors,
the flagrant air brushes its lips against
our glacier's cheek and slow retreat,
is kissing resistance goodbye.

CEREMONY

Some ceremony is involved
in hauling the bicycles up from the basement,
angling their awkwardnesses
under ductwork, around the stairwell landing,
and through the needle's eye of the side door,
as one wheel spins free, ticking.

The sun was singing down, loud and glorious,
as we wove our two thin tire-lines through town
and to the bay, then through and around surprising
numbers of walkers, strollers, roller-
bladers of varying degrees of proficiency, and other
cyclists, all of us twisting and braiding
our various momentums together
like a fat rope played out by the water's edge,

and the gravel swallowed our tires as we left the paveway
and headed toward the point, while volleyed
in and out of hearing on the wind we heard the beat
of some hydraulic jack driving posts into the earth,

or some jack's boom box, I said,

but came upon the backs of three white
T-shirts there instead, and the draped jet
hair and braids of two men and a woman
sitting facing the open blast
furnace of light on the water,
in the sky, and drumming
the sun down,

singing rhythmic undulations over
the chanted surface of the bay,

a song that went nowhere, musically,
and could have gone there forever—
                                        and the gravel
swallowed our tires again, as we quit
the landfill point to be home before dark,
and all I wanted to convey is the deep enjoyment
of our early summer evening ride, the unexpected
explosion of people at the new waterfront park
three generations after industry and E.coli
drove them all away, and the three first-peoples,
this late in the game, chanting and drumming
the sunset as an event
in which they were participant,
while we looked on.

WHITE BUFFALO JUMP

Odds are, you'd say, by now Brock Road
should have worn itself into our mindscape;
like those paths, here, that before we came
everyone walked: the centuries' generous pounding
that sank them one foot, two feet down;
and the hills really happened, so did
the rock: go around.

A year of travelling
its twelve short klicks, twice weekly, you'd say,
should have printed those barns, those houses,
the quarry and the crossroads, in sequence
on the brain. I wish. I want
history, and to ride it in my sleep.

Returning home, she tells me how it went, her summer
hour with the horses: tacking up, the outdoor ring;
oxer, bounce, cavalleti—and lately, wherever
she goes, can't help but break into canter, trot,
and jumps the white rail fence, plotting
a trail to ownership: these skills,
and something living, that much larger
than herself.
                        At twelve years old, she feels the story
resolving to a landscape
she can love,
                  that loves her desire;
but can't yet trust the hills desire
happens against, rock she must
move through,
                        and by the 7th Concession Road

we've covered such familiar ground, at speed
you could wish some wishes met

                          that youngest inner drive
or need. The conversation slows, and like someone
whose own bruised geography
has never forgiven what
they did, I raise my foot
to every floating dreamscape underneath
and gently depress, braking

                   for the four-way stop.

   Above our heads

               white buffalo, in casual
   slow stampede, move across the high blue plain.
A flat-bellied herd we chase or follow
to the jumping-off

             of one day's history.

I love this road—twice weekly: its flat beeline
that rides the unremarkable hills that
only once in twelve short klicks
reach up to grab you in
the reproductive zone,

              the intimate familiarity
that holds you to

           the ground you spring from,
as in that split-second, near lift-off
you pray the earth

          not, for pleasure,
end, ever.

THE RIVER

He came to a place, the edge of a low bluff
overlooking the wide river of a dozen western movies,
and knew immediately that he'd always wanted to cross
one of these broad prairie rivers,
with its stone and pebble shallows,
the unknown strength and depth of its middle current,

on horseback (and he was on horseback),
and he knew, just as instantly,
that he couldn't take his stuff along—
the boxes covered in white canvas tied down with rope,
that had materialized out of the corner of his eye.
If he wanted to cross he'd have to leave it all behind.

He imagined his animal entering the shallows:
hooves on stones in running water;
the possible shifting underfoot,
the steady work against a heavy, downstream pull,
and rising, perhaps, on the other side. Dripping.
Would he look back? Probably.

There was no hint of irony,
no sense this scene had played innumerable times before,
on innumerable screens, in every darkness.
He felt as though he was being provided
with a piece of information, visually:
a *You-are-here.*

That this circumstance required a decision from him
was where the moment lay.

He was happy with his dream,
and felt honoured by it.

What troubles him now, if trouble
is the word, is how the dream repeats.

St. Terra

The train leaves the station at the centre of the earth
and enters the silence
of the one who is walking the railway tracks.

Ka-chunk. Each step the walker takes
is a choice, a decision that punches through
the crust of ice that protects
the soft belly of snow
that perfects the shape of the landscape.

The alternative. Ka-chunk. Is to tread
the tightrope rail itself, silver-brown
thread, over the gorgeous
new creation snow makes, that cheers
the crossing,
                    but balance is difficult
in boots, demands a concentration
alien to the place,

                    and so the walker tramps
between the lines, piston feet
breaking surface, each footfall also breaking
silence, in sound the deep passage down
instantly absorbs,
                    the imposed
deliberation of each step slowly breaking
through, prompting him to think
massage—
                    and feels the earth relax.

He thinks to feel the earth relax

beneath this winter saunter of the tracks.
Sant ter. This pilgrimage
to the holy land of going nowhere
quick. *Saint Earth.* As though feet
performed the healing dance of fingers, hands,
up and down a human back, could coax the flow
of blood again, under the numbed wound—
the raised, halo scar of rail bed—

                              with nothing more asked
than to dare the simple intimacy of this touch.

The walker enters the giant, silent engine room of earth's centre,
stands back,
             waits
as the train whistles through the stations of snow.

BEACH

In the church where we go to now a remnant people
fan themselves with the white paper wing of the bulletin,
on which is listed their comings and goings,
events, the summer schedule.

In the church where we go to now the white wings of seagulls
float among the rafters, above the sand,
where medieval castles of childlike construction,
that weren't there yesterday
and will be gone tomorrow,
are built and rebuilt,
subject to the rhythm and eternal Love of water.
People in low chairs line the shore,
observe the unmoving line of the horizon,
the motion of waves, the slow motions of the sky,
looking for signs, signs, signs—
though really they are not looking for anything at all.
Their present situation is quite sufficient.
The rhythm and eternal Love of water drew them here,
where the land ends and their faith stretches beyond limit,
and is quite sufficient.

In the church where we go to now a man and a woman
stand knee-deep in the water, talking,
allowing the lake to take its sweet, satisfying time.
They are talking Deep Ecology, Current Fiction, or fictions.
They are talking the Desert Fathers.
A beach ball makes a dash for freedom,
launching itself across the waves with the wind,
chased by a paddler on an air mattress,
past the third sandbar.

The paddler returns, rejoicing.
In any sanctuary, indoors or out,
the inscrutable parable of our childlike lives
is open to ongoing interpretation.
A man throws a tennis ball.
His young, long-haired Labrador bounds into the waves
and swims to shore holding in his jaws the fuzzy yellow pearl
it is clear he would gladly sell everything he owns
to retrieve.

Among the animals, it is our hairlessness
that stands out. In the holy, catholic church
there is no fear or shame. The godly walk and bask
beside the rhythm and eternal Love of water.
Bellies hang bulbous over the waistbands
of men whose jewels dangle in small pouches hung below,
like stones in a slingshot.
The round tops of numberless breasts abound,
leap from their halters. All that is hidden
will one day be revealed, and the day
seems very near.

The knee-deep man and woman are still talking.
They are discussing if and how the surface tension of lake water
 might bear their everyday weight.
The wind begins to rise.
Medieval castles of air and water
begin construction on the line of the horizon,
and as the people prepare to flee the wrath foretold,
they ask, *Will the weather always be so variable*
in the church where we go to now?

The white wings of seagulls hang in the rafters
as the seagulls wait for signs.
They land, filling the spaces left vacant by the departed.
They scream their screams for the departed,
picking at the sand for any trace,
their last communion with the departed.

I remember now.
A family of four or six drives down the highway
on the last day of summer vacation, arguing and debating
where to stop to eat, where every day and meal
is a communion, one with the other,
and with the creatures of flesh who congregate the shoreline,
and with our eternal brother, who walked and basked upon
the rhythm and eternal Love of water,
that bids us, so appealingly, *Come.*

TENSION

In the church where we go to now
  a tension exists
  that has nothing to do with the setting
or a person or an issue: it just is.
Or it may have everything to do with the setting,
a particular individual, a current debate.
And as time plays on you may feel the key wind
and the string tighten
until it is stretched
to the furthest point you think it is possible to stretch
without snapping,
and perhaps this is only a personal,
internal version of that same tightrope
that the preacher walks across the natural chasm
between our hearts and the heart of God,
but winched to excess....
Don't anyone come near me,
you inwardly shout.
I'm not enjoying this anymore.
And what is this peculiar kind of torture
that you, and we, are putting ourselves through,
that you, and we, would choose it?

You're at another meeting, or out visiting,
and someone adds a word or two to the topic at hand,
which causes the air in the room to vibrate slightly,
which you attribute to your current state,
still taut as cat gut—
another responds, and then, though the effort
  is intense, you toss in
your two cents, and it isn't so much

what is said, as how, and why,
and *twang*, the relief is instantaneous.
The string has been plucked.

Ah, so this is how the music is made.

In the church where we go to now
the tension exists
of the two or three or more
who have gathered in the name of...
in the name of...
in the name of...
and the body is played as a stringed instrument:
a lute, a lyre, a harp, or, more likely,
a guitar, a piano, a violin.
And the music that is made
comes at the cost of this peculiar tuning-together
that hurts
as it readies for pleasure.

ART

In the church where we go to now
no one will object
if you were to understand the light wind
that came up a moment ago,
and has come up again, at this moment,
brushing against your skin—
if you were to take it personally,
as directed to you in particular,
this breath of air...

though some of these smaller events
are not communicable, are meant
for you alone.

In the church where we go to now
there is no grand agenda.
A thin line is stretched or strung,
neighbour to neighbour,
between the beauty of this world
and the obvious daily misery that exists next door.

Some days there is nothing wrong with the world.
Two birds, whose exact location remains a mystery,
are speaking to you, it is true,
from within the multitudinous leaves
of a single tree which has just come to life.
The wind again.
There is also the orange feathered spray
of this high-borne cirrus clouding,
at what was known, once, as the waning of the day.

A finely-rendered display,
beautiful, changing and complete.
But is it art? I mean,
is there a hand?

In the church where we go to now
four campers sit or slouch around a beach fire
beside a lake in northern Quebec.
The moon is intently illuminating the filigree of clouds,
the water is intensely reflective.
"Art is a product of human culture," one states.
Another replies, "Sky, water, rock, trees—
    it is all art, and we are part of it."

It is humanly possible to stand between
the individual drops of a light shower of rain,
to witness the damp dots paint the sidewalk
or the sand, and not be touched or struck.

The next day, the four are caught
between the water they are canoeing upon
and the water that is descending,
    ever more abundantly, from above.
Thunder booms. "This isn't fun anymore,"
shouts one from the bow,
"It's on the cusp
of sucking."

Later, at least one of the four will think
of recent stories, and people fleeing the thunder

and flashes of light that flattened their towns and cities,
in some country, somewhere on the globe,
and who are living outdoors in the mountains and woods,
the reports said,
with winter coming.

In the church where we go to now
we paddle to an inhospitable shore
for safety, and stand among and on the rocks,
hours from home, in mild desolation,
as the high, social realism of an autumn downpour
connects the dots between ourselves
and everything else that is wrong with the world,

artfully.

JAWS

People, I'm sorry.
    I didn't know until I sailed into your quiet cove
    how big the vessel is
of this anxiety.

Yesterday, on *Saturday Night at the Movies*,
we watched *Jaws*,
which I had never seen,
and now in the silences between these words
I hear the three near-strangers
drunk and singing,
    Show me the way to go home...
aboard the vessel *Orca*, and comparing scars,
as one whale of a shark
takes aim at their hull,
and I think,

    I never set out to look for a shark.
    They did, but I didn't.

They shot and shot at it.
Fat lot of good bullets do.
The one with the harpoon gun is swallowed whole,
slipping down the tipped deck
into the shark's open mouth.
Then the man from the city blows the fish to a million pieces
as their boat sinks,
and the two survivors doggy-paddle back to shore
clinging to flotsam.
Nice to know how it all turns out, but.

It only hit me as I sat inside your upturned hull
how big the vessel is
of this anxiety, the grief and fear
we only tell each other of
two or three together,
drunk as them.

Something's out there.
Show me. Show me home.

Humus

The church where we go to now
is no big deal, a small group of protesters,
half a millennium after the fact,
in a city of need
in a hurried, wasteful time:
and it seems a kind of perverse luxury
that we experience so many varieties
of grief and sorrow
made available in such abundance,
though it doesn't quite fit
with the cut of our clothing,
or the cleanliness of our skin,
with only each other to fall back on,
after all, and our only righteousness
the love we bring,
and it is not for our perfections
that we are loved,
or the perfection of our gifts,
but only that we are, all, made
for this conversation, going on,
and now, having travelled
a dark passage
into this early morning light,
our eyes adjust,
we taste a kindness in the air,
this spring we smell
difference,
we catch an ancient scent, and
Holy Scat—
Holy dog dirt on the lawn

after the snows are gone:
we've been pulled through.
We're only humus, after all.
And all the good we thought we were,
and all we did or did not do,
these seasons past,
is gone to soil, is
Holy. Holy. Holy.

LOGOS

In the church where we go to now
no one is perfect.
The preacher walks a tightrope
between our hearts and the heart of God.
Halfway across, she dances acrobatics.

In the church where we go to now someone collects string.
There are one hundred and forty-four thousand strands
tied together into a big ball, into a net, a cloth—
the ball winds labouriously uphill,
then unravels with alarming regularity, down;
the net catches the artists of high wire acts,
and hauls in fish from the other side of the boat
whether the fish like it or not,
then asks, "Do you love me?"
The cloth is a shroud
with the debated face of Jesus burned through it;
the cloth is a bright T-shirt advertising irresistible logos.

In the church where we go to now
someone falls out of a three-storey building
and lands on the hood of a car,
miraculously escaping injury;
there is a mother with three small children
    who will not live out the year.

In the church where we go to now
I saw the hands of Jesus separate the clouds of night
    and prevent the spell and curse of evil intent
    from taking hold;
I saw the bodies of family members exhumed from mass graves.

In the church where we go to now a young woman
plans a mission trip to a foreign country,
and asks for the prayers of the people;
a young man experiences headaches
that will not go away, and asks
for the prayers of the people; children
of the prayers of the people are born out of wedlock;
the unceasing prayers of the people reshape
the results of the CAT-scan
in one person's immediate future.

In the church where we go to now
people come and go.
Drought, famine, fire and ice
have reduced the population by half;
someone is suing the manufacturer,
and no one is perfect.

In the church where we go to now
there is an indescribably painful beauty
that has to do with the two edges of truth
being drawn through our lives.

One person leads their child to the edge of a small pool
that is lying perfectly still in its dish,
and asks that the water be troubled, asks
that they both be sprinkled upon.

It is the day of the Spirit.
The preacher handsprings, swings from a branch.

In the church where we go to now people go and come;
three men and a woman, two women
and two men, an infant, a teenage son
enter the cloud of witness,
they stand beneath the arms of a tree
and say, *Yes.*

SILENCE

In the church where we go to now
there are patches of silence
that open up beneath you,
and closing your eyes
you may feel your grip loosen on the wheel
as you wake to the realization
that for the past six days you've been driving
against the white noise of wind and engine,
steadily over the limit,
and like a four-lane highway
where the bridge is collapsed,
you've hit the open gap
between one minute and the next,
and suddenly you're airborne, plunged
slowly into the stream below,
but unharmed, standing in the middle of a landscape
that looks very much like early childhood;
and gazing up you see the traffic
of the previous week come diving
over the same edge, in pursuit,
but instead of burying you
in their tons of wreckage, they suffer
an inexplicable reduction in body weight,
and float down to the water
like falling leaves,
where they are gently carried downstream.

You can hear the buses on King Street
when they pass by the building; a hearing aid
pierces the stillness with its high-pitched tone;
and if the sun comes out, the solid, sheet plastic

storm windows on the inside will expand
and start crackling like flames of the Holy Ghost,
and if the dog next door catches wind
his barking punctuates the music
as the first quiet notes of the piano
begin to draw you upward again.

By the time you've returned to solid ground,
with your eyes open, singing,
you can see that you've landed on the far side
of that wide, open gap, rescued
from a disaster you didn't see coming.
But it must have been a bus you were riding
all last week, because
so many others surround you now,
everyone on foot, ready to turn
and walk, ready, as they say,
to travel down that crooked highway.

DISARMAMENT

If you sit on the third floor balcony
of your twenty-six storey apartment building downtown,
you may find yourself staring down the barrel
of a twenty-five pounder gun, a howitzer,
positioned on the front lawn of the military museum
    across the street,
and feel perfectly confident that it is disarmed,
or hope so.

We carry no weapons here.
There is a formal requirement to love
    the one who stands beside the howitzer,
whether the howitzer be disarmed or armed,
and this keeps us in constant communication
with the unseen one who stands behind the one
who tomorrow may stand poised beside the howitzer.
For there is always the part in us
that considers the defence of our own bodies
    to be in our own hands,
that would avenge injustice,
the suffering of ourselves and others,
regardless of formal requirements.

And if they come with knife or fire,
or if the gun is held to my daughter's head,
if I and mine are driven into hiding under the High Level Bridge,
fleeing roundup, awaiting the inevitable
with others of our social, religious, ethnic
    or national community,
No, I do not beforehand know what my response will be.

Our lives run through our fingers like water.
Salt or red, the liquid drops that fall from our bodies,
the bodies of others,
fall onto the heated surface of current events.
The drops suffer and dance across the surface
and are released into the air.
They rise as the unseen vapour of supplication and intercession.
Our lives are the prayer given up against a cycle of violence.
The prayer forms a cumulo-witness,
condensing under the floor of heaven.

And you who read sky and radar screen,
who understand the behaviour of wind and cloud,
the markings on overhead jets—
how is it that you cannot detect the flight of the spirit,
my brother, my twin,
or where a reconciling rain might fall?

The war is never elsewhere.
The seeds of conflict float down on parachutes,
its roots run deep as dandelions
     in the front lawn of the military museum.
Our enemy currently lives behind a door
on the seventh floor of the same downtown apartment building.
He and his friends, male and female, toss bottles,
shout up and down from balcony to ground, at all hours,
keeping us in constant communication
with the unseen one who sits beside us on our balcony,
who lies beside us in our bed, listening.
Inevitably, the volume is turned up
as they dance to further taunt his formal requirement.

Tonight we lie awake,
and invite the spirit come brood over our twenty-six storeys,
the storied conflicts of a tired world.
To tuck us under wing, all.

Come, love,
disarm us.

The Economy of Hope

I'm thinking back to the pale grey, concrete houses
of Port-au-Prince, half-walled and roofless,
their reinforcing rods waving stiffly in the atmosphere
of dust, like clipped antennae, frayed nerve ends
sticking out from unfinished second-storey floors
in the aftermath of an earthquake, a bomb;
or like the wild, shaking leaves of grass
in a basket still being woven.

But the picture in my mind is not one
from our dozens of photographs, but of Bill,
our host, sitting at the dinner table one evening,
telling us the truth is opposite these visuals,
that the houses are not, in fact, derelict,
abandoned in defeat, but "works-in-progress,
just as I am, just as we all are."

We were dining at the Beck Hotel,
where a steady traffic walked its private drive,
of people stepping through a break
in the stonewall fence, climbing a path
behind the building, up to where they lived
on the hillside,
                        behind a veil of leaves
alive with the sounds of habitation.

Bill explained that if a person saved a little money here,
and if extended family laid no prior claim,
they might invest it in a few concrete blocks,
or in a window, a door.
And though they may not live to see

their home complete,
the vision keeps.

There is much I do not understand
in the economy of hope.

The Beck was built by a couple from Germany,
as a resort stop. It survives into this time
when the cruise ship no longer docks,
complete with pool and dance patio,
run by the elderly Mr. Beck, their son,
who stopped by our table.
All the hotel furnishings, the beds, window frames, bar,
were made from mahogany trees
growing when the couple first arrived,
by a carpenter who lived on site.

And our Mr. Beck planted a forest,
and when the trees matured
he planned to retire on their harvest.
But someone came, and sawed,
and left him destitute of his investment,
and I have this vision of the forest
fanning out in single planks across the countryside,
standing on end at roadside lumberyards,
and carried past his own front door, up the hill,

or into Port-au-Prince,
and through the dusty, pale grey neighbourhood
that we toured with a nurse on her rounds.
And one plank came to lie on the bench

of a carpenter we passed,
who made from it the frame-and-panel door
that opened on a room we were invited to enter,
where lay a work-in-progress,
born just the night before.

There is much that I do not understand
in the economy of hope and perseverance.
Behind the veils of concrete, the neighbourhood
was alive with the sounds of human habitation.
Reinforcing rods waved wildly in an atmosphere
of dust weaving through the holy destitution.

CONVICTION

The preacher stands in the middle of an island
holding the world in one hand.
Today the world is orange.
It grows on a tree that grows
on a small plot of ground that is on the island.
A disciple has climbed into the tree
and dropped the orange world
to a second disciple,
who offers it to the preacher,
who stands holding in her right hand
the world, and in the left a machete.

She stands her small plot of ground, the preacher.
The blade slips under the skin
and the orange world begins to spin
as she pares.
Our fascination grows
as the latitudes unravel and dangle
a loose spiral
that disconnects from the pole and falls to earth,
and the orange world turns pulp white.

To each of us she offers just such
a soft and unprotected world,
its two hemispheres clinging together
from the knife sliced not quite through
    the equator,
which is where she lives.

To receive from her
we must accept the fruit,

the blade that she withdraws
from the world she places in our hands—
and goes to pare new worlds,
as the juice from this, her gift
and her conviction,
springs fresh to our tongues.

THREE STONES: PORT-AU-PRINCE

The general populace in their Sunday best
    (for it is Sunday)
      in bright tableau against a tiered rock wall,
receive and stoop and turn and stand, and turn
to receive again, as the plastic jugs and pails
pass hand to hand, down row by row from the top,
where, today, the tap runs clear water.

Three stones support a pot.

Three oranges (it is orange season)
support a fourth, on top of which
is balanced another, or one more.
These brilliant towers of fruit grow
beside the road, presided over by women
who balance on their haunches on this island
that is balanced on a globe,
frank and modest in their brilliant skirts.

The stone in the river does not know
the misery of the stone in the desert.

A man sits bent over a treadle sewing machine
in the shade of a sheet of corrugated steel
intensely focussed on a point, still
and moving, where his fingers have gathered
like a small crowd around a faucet.

The needle dances in place,
a pencil point lopes across a page.

[65]

The tailor is scribe to a thread
that winds through the fabric of this open
island world. We are all of us
pierced all the way through,
by the needle that is drawing this thread.

FREE LUNCH

Why is it that whenever I talk with my old professor
my eyes water, my intelligence shorts out
like a small appliance,
and my voice takes on a waver
that mimics the gentle, aging waver of his hand,
his hand as it points toward the bottle of beer:

Upper Canada Rebellion. How apt.
The tall waitress smiles as I look up
and ask for the same, in much the same way
my great-grandfather may have looked up
from the dark, tenant rows, and wondered,
Do gods smile?
                        It seems a past century
that I worked the field beneath
my retired mentor's landed mastery,
and bent to taking notes.

She returns at last. Our bottles match.
Two brown rebels: democrats.
Her height above the table, her legs
beneath a skirt. His manners, his books.
Her bare, round shoulders and her peerless chest,
upon which in normal circumstance I would not obsess,
though after three generations
I still work by hand,

                        and gladly, dammit,
as gladly as, once yearly,
I bow these luncheon respects to my better—

his learning, my lack, the waitress returning
with what he'll also command: the bill.

And remember not to lick my knife.
And nod as sagely as I dare, to him,
to her, whom I would choose to serve
and follow anywhere.

ORAL PLEASURES

Going to the Dutch Toko, you may discover
more about your mysterious self
than you knew before,
or perhaps wanted to.
                Standing at the meat counter,
ordering *boterham vorst*, the *vorst*
for *boerenkoel*, or asking one of the women
to lift a wheel of cheese
from the glass-doored cheese fridge,
which she then sets on a table
built a little too high,
so that she must stand on her toes
to put sufficient shoulder behind the curved,
two-handled knife, which slides reluctantly through
the hard *Gouda…*

                Gouda. Its half-horked g-sound
is such an oral pleasure. Here
you don't have to anglicize
in order to be understood,
as you do downtown in the Farmers' Market.
That's the first clue.

Clue two is how abruptly familiar
and exotic, both, the inside of the Toko is.
If you've lately neglected this far north-end
of the dreary indoor Mountain Plaza,
you might now recognize the place
such smells and tastes
have in the soul, not only the heart,
or the mouth, where the spiced tang

of *pepermunten*, true
as the bite of the North Sea
blowing through an open window,
is contained in the small room
of tongue and teeth,
                    and is very sweet.
How it must have changed their lives
when the shipped spices first entered
the homes of the Dutch, when nutmeg
first was grated over green beans,
or *Faam* and *King* began to spar for allegiance
in the pews...

                  though by the time these two
have sailed through the generations
to take up official residence in your soul,
all brand name quarrels have been put aside,
melting into an inconsequential sliver,
so that now, somewhere in my soul,
where I'm looking to get this right,
is the third clue,
about the size of a *Canadezen* nickel
balancing on its narrow edge:
the simple, whole white disk,
which I would ask Mom to give me one of,
just as the silver plate came by
that held the precise white squares
of crustless bread the adults held so dear
they each took only one of,
                    and gripped

between their thumb and forefinger,
waiting till everyone in that large boat of a building
had the piece they guided to their mouths,
on cue, together, in the hushed rustle
of best Sunday clothing,
then silently chewed;
contemplative, or simply blank—impossible
to say:
        thankful, penitent,
unregenerate....

                     At the Toko, they'd know.
And possibly tell you. Sometimes the women
can't help you right away, or when they do,
pay scant attention as they slip your wishes,
like a single slice of *rokvlees*
falling from the rolling guillotine,
between the *hapjes* of fresh information
they meanwhile are feeding
each other,
            but who can mind?
You're being served. Clue four
is impaled on the end of a toothpick
held between thumb and forefinger:
the sample *stukje*, salty or sweet,
that will draw, on its brief journey
through the air and to your mouth,
a shape like a question mark
to punctuate the tidbit facts
you overhear, or some richer delicacy,

imported from their's or your's or other's lives,
and which you freely, in turn,
offer and exchange, innocent
of all intent.

Such oral pleasures.

Everything comes in packages, from far away:
the wedge of *nagelkaas*, wrapped in wax paper,
and taped; *beschuit* silos, slipped in cellophane
thin as silk; the bright rolls of *Rang*.
a former paradise proffers
its arresting smells and tastes.
                              Each good
drawn from the shelves, examined
at various angles, and placed
in the wire basket, is highly valued—
and the small pile, emptied
before the cash register,
                              is very dear.

And they will always know more, here,
about your mysterious self
than you.
                  Clue five is the blue logo'd bag
with a windmill printed on it,
by which you advertise
your coming and going
along the corridor, through
the wide glass doors, where,

as you slowly flee the dreary inexcusable mall
to enter their domain,
the immigrant sun
and North Sea cloud
                    embrace
your late arrival.

POOLSIDE

Now in Jerusalem by the Sheep Gate there is a pool…
                                                    — JOHN 5

There is no water flatter, or more still,
      than the water that is contained within the blue walls
      of the randomly shaped swimming pool
at the resort hotel on a shore of the Caribbean Sea.

Lounging beside it, I recall the pool
around which the infirm would gather, waiting
for the one day of the year an angel came
to trouble its surface, and the first to enter was healed.

I have waited the better part of a long winter
to be here. Beyond the palms of this hotel
is the village of small concrete homes, flat roofs
and brightly-coloured doors that opened

to the tour bus negotiating its exceptionally
narrow streets, hauling us all from the airport.
The bus bleats, *Let me through, Let me through.*
You wouldn't have thought we could make it.

Poolside, rich imported languages blossom
like tropicals. French, Italian, German, Dutch,
and the one I dip my tongue into,
are interspersed with the occasional bleat

of goat. The goats are tied to palm trees,
under which the tour buses idle. Porters
push carts of baggage between lounge chairs,
while the angels who daily trouble our sheets

and towels to perfection, talk, and walk in twos
a straight line through to the rust buckets waiting
to return them home to the village, after shift.
The poor are with us always, and we have come

a long way to find them. The first one into the pool
is already better for it, in this heat.
The water returns to a stillness I have come
already to love. Were he to stretch a hand

and offer it, I think I could not stand
to relinquish this choice infirmity.

WILD EDIBLES

Now on that same day two of them
were going to a village called Emmaus…
—LUKE 24

They walked on dry land.
Having stepped into the current of the past week's events,
a river that over the previous three days
had upgraded itself to Class IV whitewater
before pitching them headlong over a surprise, improbable falls
that very morning,
they were still not sure exactly what had happened,
but were happy to be on dry land,
if it was dry land.
And they were blameless.

They also truly had no idea what the message said,
scrolled tightly inside the waterproof canister
each wore around his neck.
When they met him on the path,
it was the first question he asked.

It showed on their faces. Exhaustion.
What rock have you been hiding under? they wondered.

He bore no distinguishing features.
No nicks or scars, no claw marks, nothing.
He may just as well have been one very well-read park ranger,
lecturing them on their own moral and natural responsibility,
the park warnings on natural hazards,
or a backpacking, itinerant Methodist preacher
tapping in the tent pegs of his point.

Ah, his point.

Where are you from? he asked.
The city, they said.
What did you see there?
We saw the streets and avenues of justice torn up
    for sewer work, impassable, masquerading as river.
We watched a man give up his own blamelessness
    as though he were the chosen animal of these woods.
We gathered beneath a tree where he was slung,
    mourning, mingling with murderers,
until we saw that in the crowd that crowded underneath
    the two were indistinguishable,
and it hardly matters,
for we all eat.
We all must eat.

He poked a branch in their fire.
You must be hungry now, he said.
If you care to join us, they replied.

And he fed them wild edibles.
And twisting free the caps from the waterproof canisters,
he placed upon their tongues
the scrolls
that burned all the way down.

Their eyes outshining their flashlights
as he slipped away between the trees

THE EASY PART

Barbara, when Bart came by with the news,
we were taking down the garage.
You know the one, behind John and Martha's:
it's looked like a pushover for ages. Surprise.
That lilting twist along its spine, and the cockeyed
doorway that scared their car onto the drive
was only half the story. The other half
is how attached it was to living at that angle,
with no desire to fall, and no intent.

We went at the job with a sledgehammer
and three different kinds of saw, their blades
dulling almost instantly against the building's
wonderful resistance. Then there stood Bart,
beside the dumpster we'd hired, with his son,
Wesley, who is eight. Why aren't all things and creatures
granted leave to take their own sweet time,
since it's so plain love alone maintains them?

Down the street, you were packing the last boxes
of your young family's move to Montreal,
when you first learned the news.
You must have entered your new home there,
and the physical reality of Donald's death, who'd gone
ahead of you, at just about the time we manhandled
the last jagged pieces of the garage's unwilling puzzle
into the bin, and swept up.

A friend and neighbour's yard is one big open
space now. We plan to fill it, soon,
with studs and rafters, true to the other's memory.

That's the easy part. Harder is
the work of love in monstrous vacancies
the heart had never planned to open to.
We wish that we could build you something there,
to house the jagged pieces, the emptied air.

HOW IT ALL GOES ROUND

In the church where we go to now
the time has come for redefinition.
For instance: *life everlasting.*
I'd like to think eternal being involves
the rock face exposed
by the highway blasted through,
and the possibility of slipping one's new, improved
body and soul
between the seams that divide time
from time,
to land on a beach
on the evening and the morning of the third day.

Ah! Creation.
It would be good. Very good.

I'd like to think that forever and ever and ever and ever
includes entering the cycle
whereby water congregates on the horizon as medieval castle
and is deconstructed, directly overhead,
into a million and one almost identically-sized parts
that simultaneously, one after the other,
fall.
I would ride the single drop on the windshield,
in the downspout,
jump the last few inches
and slip between the particles of earth,
descending to the root of darkness,
where I might rejoin my liquid kin,
and feel our urge to well

spring into pond, creek,
and be the river
running
to embody the lake;
and await the surface touch of fire
from ninety-three million miles,
and enter our star's fire,
the burn that prompts rising
re-congregation into the middle air...

and begin again.

The one I love loves how it all goes round and round and round
the one I love is of the air, is of fire, of water, rock
dancing.

And if I am to be saved,
if my religion allows,
let it also be from this,
let me be saved from the ceaseless, unending,
eternal ways that I
and my body
constrict
in the face of this life,
which is love everlasting,
from how I and my body
gravitate, fall,
for that other lover, death.

The one I love
lives
in the air on fire under water through rock breathing liquid
molten flowing granite flames forever and ever and ever and ever
lasting.

Ah! Creation.

The one I love
The one I
The one

Two Couples, Four Voices

1. THE CARPENTER MEDITATES ON HIS CONDITION

Before the man was a husband
he looked to his bride-to-be.
Who is the father? he asked.
This child, she said, is from God.

Before the man was a husband
he lay awake in his bed,
thinking of his betrothed, his bride-to-be,
as he often did, though differently now that the child Christ,
whom he did not know as the child Christ,
was already creating a visible bulge.
The man asked himself:
    Can I go through with this?
    What will be the social fallout?
    Is what I am feeling called humiliation, or shame?
    To whom is my primary responsibility?
The man rolled around on his bed
    tossing questions like tennis balls against the wall,
and it were best to his mind, he concluded,
    that she go away, quietly.

Before the man was a husband he slept
the sleep of the righteous, having made a decision.
But his sleep did not lead him beside still waters,
nor did it place him on the other side of this peculiar night,
which he found was growing deeper within him.
And it began to seem to the man
that he was told it was so, not asked:

the light that came through the window
was too bright to mistake it, the voice
too clear to his soul. The voice
awakened something in his soul
(the soul understood as the self's awareness of itself)
that did not wish to be awakened.
It awakened the longing for return
that had lain in his soul from the time
    when he first began to walk, and the earth was young,
from the time he first spied the fruit
    but could not unbite what he had bitten,
when he saw his brother fall beneath his hand
    and could not wash the stain away from his hand.
He ran and hid his nakedness.
In the cool of the evening, the Maker walked near,
    calling to him, Where are you?
I am afraid, and I am hiding, the man said.
Who told you that you were naked? the Maker asked.
The woman you gave me... said the man.

Could this be the return that the man longed for?
He was naked again, lying in his bed,
    and thinking of his betrothed.
He was afraid again, but not so much.

Before the man was a husband his heart returned
to his betrothed, his bride-to-be, who was showing.

I am not the father.
I am not the father.
I am not the father.

This child comes from God.

Is there ever an instance, the man thought,
is there ever an instance where this statement is not true?

2. MARY, FACING FACTS

When the bride-to-be first told her future husband the news
she sat on the couch, afraid.
He asked her point-blank, and she cried,
but the weight that she had carried thus far alone
was lifted instantly, and the immense relief she felt
at having unburdened herself
produced a half-smile on her lips,
a smile which, to his credit, the man did not interpret wrongly.

In her mind the young, unmarried mother-to-be understood
that to be expectant suggested anticipation, joy.
All the books that she had not yet read said so.
The books had not been written yet.
The books had not yet been written
that would tell the life story of the hero—
if we may call him that—
who was still only an indecipherable hieroglyphic
on the opening pages of her life.
Perhaps if she were to read the last chapter first
in one of those books,
if she knew how the story ended…
Would she still wish to carry through to full-term?
At this point all her options seemed to lead through pain.

Before the bride-to-be was a bride she carried a child.
Who would believe her report?
The child, when it was born, would be known,
    in the common usage of the time,
as her son, not his—
neither the His with a capital H,
nor the his of the not-father-to-be, in the lower case.
Stories other than the stories later to be written
    would circulate.
They already were.
The child would begin life at the very bottom rung
    of the communal ladder.
She could provide no high birth for the Prince of Light—
what other names had the messenger written
on the slowly growing hill
under where her warm hand now rested?
He will be called names other than Prince of Peace.

And yet, to be joyless,
even in her condition,
would be as if to punish the child,
who himself had done no violence, nor sin.

He will be known as his mother's son.
Why is this a form of curse?
He will be mine in name only.
I sense the beginning of suffering.
He is not yet born, and yet I miss him.
I feel the shaft that pierces my heart.

3. ELIZABETH, SWELLING

She was a bulbous, billowing old vessel of flesh.
She was Sarah-the-second-time-round.
She was too old for this,
and she was not laughing.
Actually, she was laughing.
For it was outrageous and absurd and wondrous to behold
her wrinkled skin stretched tight and smooth over her belly.
She was in love with the new geography of her old body,
with the hill rising in her middle distance.

Have you ever felt good for nothing,
an example of total inadequacy, utter uselessness,
a burden to yourself and others—
it would have been better had you never been born?
That had been her experience.

Concerning the man, she had wondered:
Do they feel redundant to, and excluded from,
    the process of creation,
and does this influence their behaviour?
Is it because they resent and fear a woman's ability
    to create human life in the first place,
or the attention a woman must focus
    solely upon the mystery of her own body,
that they turn so sullen when there is no child?

She was a bulbous, billowing old vessel of flesh,
whose husband of many years had looked upon her,
for many years,

as the sole agent of their childlessness.
He had retreated into an inner sanctum of his own creation,
a dense silence from which he could not be coaxed or humoured.
She imagined him in the closet, praying:
    The woman you gave me.
    The woman you gave me. Lord.
    The woman you gave me. Lord. Oh Lord.

The injustice of it had pursued her almost to her grave.
But now this! The sweet outlandishness,
the biological implausibility!
She relished what she understood as a divine irony:
herself swelling like a watermelon in the sun,
him dancing around her, near bursting,
wanting to speak, to shout, to sing, but unable.
She detected a godly humour
    that completely disarmed her need for justice.
She floated in a sea of forgiving forgetfulness,
feeling herself so well-remembered.
She sensed the beginning of the end of suffering.

And what of the fact that thirty years in the future
the head of her grown son, soft under the hill
    upon which her warm hand lay today,
would be presented on a platter, severed from the body
    that at this moment was forming within her?
All things remain in God.
Each day has enough sorrow for itself.
By then, she knew, she would be sleeping with her ancestors,
pleased to be rejoined by the child of her old age.

4. THE TEMPLE RAT SCRATCHES HIS RESPONSE
ON BOTH SIDES OF THE PAPER

I am an old man and a young father.
There's the riddle:
how and why the rules of nature were bent,
and the code by which I governed my life
turned and twisted
like a New York City sidewalk pretzel.

I am a happy old gourd of a man
with a babe in arms.
Once, to hold a son in my arms meant the world to me.
There were religious as well as personal considerations.
I stood with the match burning in my hand
to light the incense of unceasing prayer
when the messenger met me with the news.
People were waiting.
If I hadn't stammered then, asking him
to prove himself, to flash
his angelic credentials,
I might be speaking to you now.
But who can blame me?

I was a dutiful, frightened old temple codger,
caught off-guard, who asked the wrong question
and was dropped into a silence
deeper than the silence that exists, at times,
between a husband and wife.
And we are long married,
this aged young mother and I.

But in these months since my mouth was clamped shut,
I have been privileged to witness the swelling
    of my old mate's belly,
and the invisible stitching together of a human life
within the tent of another human being, a woman,
and I see now that the only true response to such a mystery
is the stunned, dumb wonder I was sentenced to.
Such is the grace shown this senior citizen.

I am a humbled, grateful old ethno-religious coot.
The questions remain the same:
Does it make any difference that I hold in my arms
    a son and not a daughter?
Is the continuation of a family name,
    and the unbroken flow of bloodlines
    through the generations,
    vital?
Am I more precious in the eye of the Maker of Life
    by virtue of my social, religious, ethnic
    or national community?

These questions have I laid upon the altar of my youth
    and old age,
against the uncertainties of time and living.
The answer reliably always was *yes*.
I am a rejuvenated old bag of bones.
The *Yes* I hear now wells with a benevolence
beyond my imagination.
It is a gift.
An elderly couple pushes the pram of their firstborn
    down the city street.

It is a gift.
They stop to buy a hot pretzel from a sidewalk vendor.
Keep the change, they say, keep the change.
It is a gift.
You are the father? the vendor asks,
and I can see that God has traded us one scandal for another.
I behave as a father.
I accept the responsibility of a father.
Am I the father?

This child comes from God.

We stand in the first drops of a rain that will become a river.
My child, who does not yet crawl, already stands within it.

You may pick your dropped jaws from the floor.
The child's name is as its mother said.
Its name is who the child is.
Its name is *Gift-of-God*.

ACKNOWLEDGEMENTS

Poems in this collection have previously appeared in *Antigonish Review*, *Dreamcatcher* (UK), *Gaspereau Review*, *Grain*, the *Hamilton Spectator*, *Image* (US), *Mars Hill Review* (US), *Malahat Review* and *Kairos*. "Giants," "Ceremony," and "St. Terra" appeared in *Falling into Place* (Gaspereau Press, 2002). "Restoration," "Planetary Lives," and "Saying Goodnight" were first published under the title *Restoration*, by Gaspereau Press as item No. 1 in The Devil's Whim occasional chapbook series. "Free Lunch" was published in *Hugh Anson-Cartwright Bookseller· A Celebration* (St. Thomas Poetry Series, Toronto; 2000.) "Beach," "Disarmament," "How it all goes round," and "Saying Goodnight" were recorded for the CD *Nod Me In, Shake Me Out*, read by the author, accompanied by Bart Nameth, with other musicians. "Two Couples, Four Voices" was developed into "A Cantata for Advent," for narrators, soloists, choir and keyboard, with additional words by the author, and music by Robert G. Rivers. The Cantata was first performed at Welcome Inn and St. Cuthbert's Presbyterian Church, in Hamilton, Ontario, in 1999. ¶ Sydling St. Nicholas is a village in Dorset, England; Sydling Water is the stream that runs through the village. ¶ The preacher in "Conviction" is not truly a preacher but rather a young health agent whose work in and around a small village in Haiti inspired the communal purchase of a piece of property. Her and the community's next goal was a medical clinic for the site. ¶ *Toko* in "Oral Pleasures" is an Indonesian word for "corner store." The other italicized words are Dutch, and for the most part are food-related: sausage (*vorst*), kale (*boerenkoel*), smoked meat (*rokvlees*), etc. *Faam* and *King* are brand names for peppermints (*pepermunten*), *Rang* for a type of fruit candy in a roll. *Hapjes* and *stukjes* are small bites, or pieces. *Nagelkaas* is a kind of cheese, studded with nails, *nagels*, ie. whole cloves, that perhaps only a Frisian can truly appreciate. ¶ Thanks to Frank deMaio,

Trevor Hamoen, Chris Jamieson, Estelle Joubert, Aaron
McCluskey, Brayden McCluskey, Glenn Macdonald, Jacob Moon,
Bart Nameth, Rudy Neufeld, Vic Neufeld, Marvin Oldejans, Matt
Posthumus, Doug Romanow, Ron Service, Leanne Tees and Marta
Vander Marel—for their musical accompaniment to the reading
of many of these, and other, poems; to Annette Abma, Jeffery
Donaldson, Scott Innes, Sue Koziey-Kronas, Maggi Martineau,
Marjonneke, Leanne Tees and Mary Terpstra—for their reading
voices; to Cathy Stewart-Kroeker, for the re-wording of one
particular line; to Linda Frank, Marilyn Pilling and Bernadette
Rule, for their particular attention to many words and lines; to
Peter Enneson for the design of most of the chapbooks and of the
CD; to Bill and Marta Vander Marel—they know why; and to
Andrew & Gary (and Beth and all the labourers in the vineyard
of word and paper) at Gaspereau Press.

Typeset in Amethyst by Andrew Steeves and printed offset at
Gaspereau Press by Gary Dunfield and Marilyn MacIntyre.
Amethyst is a typeface designed in four weights by Jim Rimmer
at the Rimmer Type Foundry, New Westminster, BC.

Gaspereau Press acknowledges the support of the Canada Council
for the Arts and the Nova Scotia Department of Tourism and Culture.

3   5   4

NATIONAL LIBRARY OF CANADA CATALOGUING IN PUBLICATION

Terpstra, John
Disarmament / John Terpstra.

Poems.
ISBN 1-894031-73-3

I. Title.

PS8589.E75D58 2003   C811'.54   C2003-903718-5

GASPEREAU PRESS ❧ PRINTERS & PUBLISHERS
ONE CHURCH AVENUE, KENTVILLE, NOVA SCOTIA
CANADA B4N 2M7